Cognitive Convergence: The Intersection of Human and Artificial Intelligence

Table of Contents

Cognitive Convergence: The Intersection of Human and Artificial Intelligence 1

Cognitive Convergence: The Intersection of Human and Artificial Intelligence 5

Table of Contents 6

Chapter 1: Exploring the Human Brain and Machine Interaction: An Introduction 7

Chapter 2: Exploring the Wonders of the Human Brain 12

Chapter 3: Machine Intelligence: Unleashing Possibilities and Overcoming Limitations 18

Chapter 4: Unleashing the Dynamic Force of Machines 24

Chapter 5: Exploring the Multifaceted Realm of Human-Machine Interaction 28

Chapter 6: Harmonizing Machine Intelligence and Human Intelligence 33

Chapter 7: The Evolving Landscape of Intelligence: Embracing Synergy and Coexistence 38

Chapter 8: Synergy through Collaboration 43

Chapter 9: Unleashing the Transformative Power: The Social Impact of Human-Machine Collaboration 48

Chapter 10: Ethical Reflections 53

Chapter 11: The Evolution of Human-Machine Collaboration: Unveiling a New Era of Interaction 58

We have got this brain, after all what is this thing! Have we got a power in the form of this brain! How does our brain remember so many things at once? How does it store so much knowledge inside itself? After all our brain can remember so many things and memories. What is this thing, have we got our brain as a gift! What is in our brain, how much information is stored together!

If it is seen properly, our brain is a huge ocean of memory and knowledge. Our brain has the capability to store more than two million gigabytes digital memory. A human brain can be updated daily with 34 gigabytes of information and also it can store in itself. Our brain is also a kind of machine. Our brain has also the ability to do all the things that a machine can do. Human brain is no less than a machine.

Out of all the parts of our body, our brain is an essential and important organ. If we didn't have a brain, we wouldn't be able to do anything, we wouldn't be living life and in fact we wouldn't be there in this world. But this doesn't mean that except the brain, all the other organs in our body are useless, they are of no use. For us to work and stay alive, only the brain is not enough. Some other organs are also important. Because our body can't be made only from the brain. All the organs are needed somewhere. All do their work properly in their places. Yes, even without some organs a person can survive on this world. But the functions of these organs do are also related to the brain.

The brain is a most important part of our body, without it no other organs can function properly. It is very important for the brain to know the news of all the work that the rest of the organs do. When the brain will know all the things of other organs, then only then the brain will keep giving us information and keep alerting. And when our brain is healthy and working properly then we will also be healthy and cool.

What does our body need, whether all the work is being done properly or not. Whether any organ has been damaged, all this brain knows, only then will it be able to work properly. And if any part is not working properly, then the brain will think about it.

For example: when we don't get enough sleep then how can we not do any work properly throughout the day, we do not feel good to do any type of work. Due to lack of sleep, all this happen to us because when we sleep, our brain also sleeps along with us. When we feel tired it is because our brain is also tired at that time. Our brain also needs to be recharged. That's why when we take rest our brain also takes rest.

This can also be understood in a way: When we see a dream while sleeping, if something is written then we are not able to read, write and speak. But it's not true in every situation, but we can identify what someone is saying or any person is attacking or anything is happening in our dreams, but we can't pinpoint the exact word or the thing.

That's why in order to be healthy, it is necessary for our brain to be healthy too.

When our mind is good, we will also be good. Whether our mood is good or bad depends on our mind too. That's why we should always take care of our brain. We will be able to take care of ourselves only if we do not neglect taking care of our brain at all. Our brain is also like a huge hole which needs to be filled with knowledge of new things all the time. We should always keep updating our brain with some new things.

Our brain is always ready to know about new things, it is hungry for gaining more knowledge about anything. When we feed it some information about new things then it gets boosted again. Then it feels good ad Start working properly. It can be understood by the help of a simple example which is described below.

When we are very hungry and then very tasty food comes in front of us and when we eat full stomach then how good we have felt at that time. Similarly, when our brain is hungry and we feed it the knowledge of new things, then it also feels good and after getting knowledges it gets boosted. As long as good things are taught to the mind, it is fine. But when a single wrong thing sits inside the brain, then that wrong thing doesn't let the brain leave it so easily. That is why we should thoughtfully put the knowledge of new things or anything in our mind. Because our brain can remember anything for a long time.

A human brain is also a type of machine. All the machines are here, all have been made by man. Then how can a machine smarter than a human? This machine which man has made, has also been made because of the human brain. Man put his mind, only then he was able to make the machine. When a machine made by man has so many features, it can store so many things, knowledge and information in it, then it is just a machine. So, then the person who has made it can be so intelligent, how many knowledge and information can be stored in him.

One thing is very good in the machine that even if any wrong thing is stored in it, then it can be easily removed from it. But once a wrong thing has captured the human mind, the thing doesn't leave the human mind easily nor does it allow it to leave the mind. Being so powerful of mind is as important for our body, it is equally dangerous too. But our brain cannot remain hollow, it has to keep feeding something or other. Just keep in mind what we are putting in the mind, the information we are giving is good information or wrong thing we are feeding our brain. We must check everything once before putting it in mind.

The human brain is always hungry for new information and knowledge. Once if it has seen or heard something and that too half, it doesn't rest until it gets complete information about that thing. There's so much capacity in our brain that whatever the knowledge aur information it acquires, the brain feels it less. Yes, our brain has so much ability, but it also desperately needs rest. If we think that the brain is always hungry for the knowledge and information all the time and just keep putting more and more things without giving a break to the mind then the mind will stop working.

The brain needs both exercise and rest. It will not work properly with only one of these two things, for that both are necessary. Human mind is such a thing, even if it doesn't exercise and keeps on resting only then it will become lazy and will not be ready to do any work. If it continues to work all the time, even if it doesn't rest at all, it will become weak and will not be able to work properly. So, our brain to stay healthy and function properly, both exercise and rest are needed.

If both the exercise and the rest of the mind are done properly, then it will be completely healthy and will be able to do all the work properly. Then man will use his brain and make a much more powerful and intelligent machine. And that machine will be very powerful and intelligent because after all this brain must have been used to make that machine.

Then who will be called more powerful, wiser and smarter; machine or human brain?

Although technology has made a lot of progress, but behind it also the contribution of human mind is there.

Let's get into it in depth!

Cognitive Convergence: The Intersection of Human and Artificial Intelligence

Table of Contents

1. Exploring the Human Brain and Machine Interaction: An Introduction
2. Exploring the Wonders of the Human Brain
3. Machine Intelligence: Unleashing Possibilities and Overcoming Limitations
4. Unleashing the Dynamic Force of Machines
5. Exploring the Multifaceted Realm of Human-Machine Interaction
6. Harmonizing Machine Intelligence and Human Intelligence
7. The Evolving Landscape of Intelligence: Embracing Synergy and Coexistence
8. Synergy through Collaboration
9. Unleashing the Transformative Power: The Social Impact of Human-Machine Collaboration
10. Ethical Reflections
11. The Evolution of Human-Machine Collaboration: Unveiling a New Era of Interaction

Chapter 1: Exploring the Human Brain and Machine Interaction: An Introduction

In this introductory chapter, we embark on a fascinating exploration of the human brain and its comparison to machines. As humans, we possess an incredible organ that enables us to think, reason, and create. But in an age of advancing technology, we find ourselves questioning the capabilities of machines and their potential to mimic or even surpass human cognitive abilities.

The human brain is a marvel of evolution, consisting of billions of interconnected neurons that work in harmony to process information and facilitate our complex behaviours. It is responsible for our perception of the world, our emotions, memories, and our ability to learn and adapt. Throughout history, humans have made significant strides in understanding the brain, unraveling its mysteries bit by bit. However, despite all our knowledge, the human brain remains a vast frontier that we are yet to fully comprehend.

With the advent of computers and artificial intelligence (AI), scientists and researchers have sought to replicate the remarkable abilities of the human brain. Machines, in their various forms, have become increasingly sophisticated, capable of performing tasks that were once solely the domain of humans. They can process massive amounts of data, recognize patterns, make decisions, and even exhibit some form of learning. This progress has sparked a debate about the limits of machines and their potential to rival or surpass human intelligence.

The field of AI has seen remarkable advancements in recent years. Machine learning algorithms, neural networks, and deep learning techniques have enabled computers to achieve impressive feats. They can now recognize faces, understand natural language, play complex games, and even generate creative content. However, despite these achievements, machines still fall short in many aspects compared to human cognition.

One fundamental difference between human brains and machines lies in their underlying architecture. The human brain is a complex network of neurons that communicate through electrochemical signals. This intricate web allows for parallel processing and the integration of information from multiple sources. On the other hand, computers operate on a binary system, processing information through logical operations performed by transistors. While computers can perform calculations at an incredible speed, they lack the inherent flexibility and adaptability of the human brain.

Furthermore, human cognition encompasses more than just logical reasoning and problem-solving. Our emotions, intuition, and creativity play integral roles in our decision-making processes. These aspects of human intelligence are difficult to replicate in machines, as they require an understanding of subjective experiences and the ability to navigate the complexities of human emotions.

However, it would be remiss to underestimate the potential of machines. As technology continues to advance, researchers are exploring new avenues to bridge the gap between human and machine intelligence. Cognitive computing, for instance, seeks to develop systems that can mimic human thought processes by combining reasoning, learning, and language understanding. By drawing inspiration from the brain's architecture and neural networks, scientists aim to create machines that can emulate human-like cognition.

In this book, we will delve deep into the intricate workings of the human brain and explore the frontiers of machine intelligence. We will examine the similarities and differences between human cognition and artificial intelligence, highlighting the areas where machines excel and where they still fall short. We will discuss the latest advancements in AI and the challenges that researchers face in their quest to develop more human-like machines.

The human brain and machines are two extraordinary entities that have captivated the imagination of scientists, philosophers, and thinkers for centuries. Each possesses its own remarkable capabilities, and together they represent the cutting edge of human knowledge and technological advancement. The human brain, with its intricate structure and vast neural networks, is the epicenter of human intelligence and consciousness. On the other hand, machines, powered by sophisticated algorithms and artificial intelligence, have revolutionized industries and transformed the way we live and work. In this exploration, we will delve into the fascinating world of the human brain and machines, examining their individual intricacies and the potential they hold when combined.

The human brain is a marvel of nature, containing approximately 86 billion neurons that communicate with each other through complex electrical and chemical signals. It is responsible for an astonishing range of functions, including perception, cognition, emotion, and decision-making. Through the interplay of various brain regions, we are capable of language, creativity, problem-solving, and self-awareness. The brain's plasticity allows it to adapt and change throughout our lives, forming new connections and rewiring itself in response to learning and experiences.

Despite the immense complexity of the brain, we are still far from fully understanding its intricacies. Neuroscientists continue to unravel its mysteries, striving to comprehend how the physical structure of the brain gives rise to consciousness and higher-order cognitive abilities. Advances in brain imaging techniques, such as functional magnetic resonance imaging (fMRI) and electroencephalography (EEG), have provided valuable insights into brain function. However, the inner workings of the brain remain largely elusive.

In recent years, the rapid progress of machines and artificial intelligence has opened up new possibilities for augmenting human capabilities and understanding the brain. Machine learning algorithms, inspired by the neural networks of the brain, have revolutionized fields such as image and speech recognition, natural language processing, and data analysis. By processing vast amounts of data and recognizing patterns, machines can make predictions, optimize outcomes, and perform tasks that were once the domain of human expertise.

The intersection of human brain research and machine learning has given rise to a new field known as neuroinformatics. Neuroinformatics aims to integrate data from various sources, such as brain imaging, genetics, and behavioral experiments, to develop comprehensive models of brain function. These models can then be used to improve our understanding of neurological disorders, develop new treatments, and even enhance human cognitive abilities.

One of the most promising applications of neuroinformatics lies in brain-computer interfaces (BCIs). BCIs establish a direct communication pathway between the brain and an external device, allowing individuals to control machines or prosthetic limbs using their thoughts. This technology holds great potential for individuals with motor disabilities, enabling them to regain mobility and independence. Moreover, BCIs have shown promise in advancing our understanding of the brain and providing insights into how neural networks encode information and produce actions.

As we explore the synergies between the human brain and machines, ethical considerations come to the forefront. The rapid development of artificial intelligence raises concerns about privacy, security, and the potential impact on employment and social structures. Ethical frameworks and guidelines must be established to ensure that these powerful technologies are developed and deployed responsibly, with a focus on benefitting humanity as a whole.

In conclusion, the human brain and machines represent two extraordinary entities that continue to shape our understanding of the world and push the boundaries of human potential. The complexity of the human brain, with its intricate neural networks and cognitive abilities, is a constant source of fascination and exploration. Simultaneously, the advancements in machine learning and artificial intelligence offer us new tools to enhance our understanding of the brain and create innovative applications that improve the quality of human life. By combining the strengths of both the human brain and machines, we have the potential to unlock a future where human capabilities are augmented, and our understanding of the brain's inner workings is vastly expanded. It is an exciting time to witness the symbiotic relationship between the human brain and machines and the transformative impact it will have on our society.

As we embark on this journey, it is important to approach the topic with an open mind. While machines have made significant progress, the complexity and richness of human cognition remain unparalleled. However, as technology evolves, the boundaries between human and machine intelligence may continue to blur. By studying and understanding both the strengths and limitations of these two domains, we can gain insights that will shape the future of AI and its impact on society.

So, join me as we navigate the intriguing landscape of human and machine intelligence, exploring the fascinating capabilities of the human brain and the ever-evolving realm of artificial intelligence. Let us embark on this intellectual adventure together, as we strive to unravel the mysteries of cognition and ponder the potential of machines to surpass our own abilities.

Chapter 2: Exploring the Wonders of the Human Brain

To truly appreciate the debate between the human brain and machines, we must first delve into the intricacies of the human brain. In this chapter, we will explore its structure, functions, and the remarkable complexity that underlies our cognitive processes. From neurons firing to the complexities of memory and emotions, we will unravel the mysteries of our most extraordinary asset.

The human brain is an extraordinary organ, weighing only about three pounds but containing billions of neurons interconnected in a complex web. Neurons are the building blocks of the brain, specialized cells that transmit electrical signals, enabling communication throughout the nervous system. These signals, known as action potentials, travel along the neurons' axons, which are long, slender projections. At the end of each axon, there are synapses, tiny gaps where information is transmitted to other neurons through chemical messengers called neurotransmitters.

This intricate network of neurons allows the brain to process information and control our thoughts, emotions, and behaviours. But how does it all work? Let's take a closer look.

At the most basic level, the brain can be divided into three major parts: the forebrain, the midbrain, and the hindbrain. Each of these regions serves different functions and contributes to our overall cognitive abilities.

The forebrain, the largest and most complex part of the brain, is responsible for higher-order thinking, decision-making, and complex cognitive processes. It includes the cerebral cortex, which is divided into two hemispheres, left and right, and is associated with various functions. The cerebral cortex is further divided into four lobes: the frontal lobe, parietal lobe, temporal lobe, and occipital lobe. Each lobe plays a crucial role in different aspects of cognition, such as executive functions, sensory perception, language processing, and visual processing.

Deep within the forebrain lies the limbic system, which is involved in emotions, motivation, and memory. It includes structures such as the amygdala, which plays a key role in processing emotions, and the hippocampus, which is essential for the formation and retrieval of memories.

Moving to the midbrain, we find structures that regulate basic functions such as sleep, arousal, and motor control. The midbrain also contains the substantia nigra, a region involved in the production of dopamine, a neurotransmitter that plays a crucial role in reward and movement.

Finally, the hindbrain is responsible for vital functions such as breathing, heart rate, and coordination of motor movements. It consists of the cerebellum, which plays a critical role in motor control and coordination, and the brainstem, which connects the brain to the spinal cord and controls basic bodily functions.

But the structure of the brain is just the beginning. What truly sets the human brain apart is its ability to process information and perform complex cognitive tasks. This is where the concept of neural networks comes into play.

Neural networks in the brain are interconnected clusters of neurons that work together to process information and perform specific functions. These networks form the basis of our cognitive abilities, allowing us to perceive the world, think critically, solve problems, and engage in creative endeavours.

One remarkable aspect of the brain is its plasticity, the ability to reorganize and adapt its structure and function in response to experiences and learning. This phenomenon, known as neuroplasticity, allows the brain to continuously grow and change throughout our lives. It is the basis for our ability to learn new skills, form memories, and recover from brain injuries.

Memory, in particular, is a fascinating cognitive function that relies on the intricate interplay of various brain regions. Memories are not stored in a single location but are distributed throughout the brain. The hippocampus, which we mentioned earlier, plays a vital role in the formation of new memories, while other brain regions, such as the prefrontal cortex, are involved in the retrieval and consolidation of memories.

Emotions, too, are an essential aspect of human cognition. They arise from the interplay of various brain regions, including the amygdala, the prefrontal cortex, and the insula. Emotions influence our decision-making processes, social interactions, and overall well-being.

As we uncover the complexities of the human brain, we come to realize that it is not merely a collection of neurons and synapses but a dynamic and intricate system that gives rise to our unique cognitive abilities. The brain's remarkable capacity for information processing, learning, and adaptation is what sets us apart from machines.

The human brain, a complex and intricate organ, has been a subject of fascination and exploration for centuries. It is the center of human intelligence, consciousness, and the driving force behind our thoughts, emotions, and actions. The study of the brain, known as neuroscience, has made significant strides in unraveling its mysteries, yet much of its inner workings remain unknown. In this exploration, we will delve into the intricate world of the human brain, examining its structure, functions, and the remarkable ways it enables us to perceive and interact with the world.

At its core, the human brain is composed of approximately 86 billion neurons, interconnected through an intricate network of synapses. Neurons are specialized cells that transmit electrical and chemical signals, allowing for communication within the brain and throughout the body. The brain is divided into various regions, each responsible for specific functions and interconnected through complex pathways. These regions include the cerebral cortex, which is associated with higher cognitive functions, the limbic system, involved in emotions and memory, and the brainstem, controlling vital functions like breathing and heartbeat.

One of the key features of the brain is its remarkable plasticity. The brain has the ability to adapt and reorganize its structure and function in response to experiences, learning, and environmental changes. This plasticity allows for the formation of new neural connections, the strengthening or weakening of existing ones, and the rewiring of circuits. It is through this dynamic process that we acquire new skills, memories are formed, and the brain continuously evolves throughout our lives.

The brain's functions are diverse and encompass a wide range of cognitive processes. Sensation and perception, for instance, enable us to perceive and interpret the world through our senses. Vision, hearing, touch, taste, and smell all rely on the brain's ability to process and integrate sensory information. This integration occurs through specialized regions of the brain, such as the visual cortex, auditory cortex, and somatosensory cortex, which extract and analyse sensory data, allowing us to make sense of our surroundings.

Cognition, another fundamental aspect of brain function, encompasses processes such as attention, memory, language, and problem-solving. The prefrontal cortex, located in the frontal lobe of the brain, plays a crucial role in executive functions, which involve planning, decision-making, and self-control. The hippocampus, a structure within the limbic system, is crucial for the formation and retrieval of memories. Language processing involves a distributed network of brain regions, including Broca's area and Wernicke's area, which are responsible for speech production and comprehension, respectively.

Emotions, too, are intricately linked to the brain. The limbic system, which includes the amygdala and the hippocampus, plays a vital role in emotional processing. These regions help regulate our emotional responses and are involved in the formation and recall of emotional memories. The brain's reward system, centred on the nucleus accumbens, is responsible for the experience of pleasure and motivation, reinforcing behaviours necessary for survival.

Understanding the brain goes beyond studying its structure and functions; it also involves investigating the mechanisms underlying neurological disorders. Disorders such as Alzheimer's disease, Parkinson's disease, schizophrenia, and depression pose significant challenges to individuals and society as a whole. Through extensive research, scientists strive to unravel the underlying causes of these conditions, seeking to develop effective treatments and interventions. Neuroimaging techniques, such as fMRI and EEG, offer valuable insights into the altered brain activity associated with various neurological disorders, aiding in diagnosis and treatment planning.

Advancements in technology have significantly contributed to our understanding of the brain. Techniques like brain imaging and electrophysiology allow researchers to study brain activity in real-time and observe how different regions communicate and coordinate their functions. Animal studies, genetic research, and computational modelling also play crucial roles in advancing our understanding of the brain.

However, it is important to acknowledge that despite the progress made, there is still much to uncover about the human brain. Its complexity, intricacy, and the sheer number of neurons and connections make it a formidable challenge to fully comprehend. The emerging field of connectomics aims to map the brain's neural connections comprehensively, providing a detailed understanding of its wiring and how it contributes to cognition and behaviour.

In conclusion, the human brain remains one of the most remarkable and enigmatic organs in existence. Its intricate structure, vast neural networks, and astonishing capabilities continue to captivate scientists and researchers worldwide. Our understanding of the brain has expanded significantly, but there is still much to discover and explore. Through continued research, innovative technologies, and interdisciplinary collaborations, we inch closer to unraveling the complexities of the human brain and unlocking the mysteries that lie within.

In the next chapter, we will shift our focus to machines and artificial intelligence, exploring their capabilities and limitations in comparison to the human brain. By understanding the fundamental differences between human cognition and machine intelligence, we can gain insights into the ongoing debate and explore the potential for machines to mimic or surpass human cognitive abilities.

So, join me as we continue this journey, unraveling the mysteries of the human brain and venturing into the realm of artificial intelligence. Together, we will explore the frontiers of human and machine intelligence, seeking a deeper understanding of our cognitive prowess and the ever-evolving landscape of technological advancements.

Chapter 3: Machine Intelligence: Unleashing Possibilities and Overcoming Limitations

In the previous chapter, we explored the intricate workings of the human brain, marveling at its complexity and ability to process information. Now, let us shift our focus to machines and delve into the realm of artificial intelligence (AI). We will examine the capabilities and limitations of machine intelligence, comparing it to the extraordinary cognitive abilities of the human brain.

Machines, in their various forms, have become an integral part of our lives. From computers and smartphones to sophisticated AI systems, they have revolutionized the way we live, work, and communicate. But what exactly is artificial intelligence?

Artificial intelligence is a broad field that encompasses the development of systems capable of performing tasks that typically require human intelligence. These tasks include perception, reasoning, learning, problem-solving, and decision-making. AI systems are designed to process vast amounts of data, recognize patterns, and make predictions or recommendations based on that data.

One of the key components of AI is machine learning, a subset of AI that focuses on enabling machines to learn from data and improve their performance over time without being explicitly programmed. Machine learning algorithms can analyse large datasets, detect patterns, and make predictions or classifications based on the learned patterns. This ability has led to significant advancements in areas such as image and speech recognition, natural language processing, and even autonomous vehicles.

Deep learning, a subset of machine learning, has garnered particular attention in recent years. It involves the use of neural networks, inspired by the structure and function of the human brain, to process and analyse data. Deep learning algorithms can learn hierarchical representations of data, allowing them to extract features at multiple levels of abstraction. This has led to breakthroughs in areas such as image and speech recognition, language translation, and even generating realistic content such as images or text.

Indeed, machines have made remarkable strides in replicating certain aspects of human cognition. They can process and analyse vast amounts of data at incredible speeds, far surpassing human capabilities. Machine learning algorithms can detect subtle patterns in data that humans may miss, leading to improved accuracy in various tasks.

Furthermore, machines can perform repetitive tasks with great precision and consistency, without succumbing to fatigue or distractions. This has proven invaluable in areas such as manufacturing, data analysis, and customer service, where efficiency and accuracy are paramount.

However, despite these impressive achievements, machines still have limitations that set them apart from the human brain. While machines excel in data processing and analysis, they often struggle with tasks that come naturally to humans, such as common-sense reasoning, creativity, and emotional intelligence.

Common-sense reasoning refers to our ability to make logical deductions based on our understanding of the world and prior knowledge. Humans can effortlessly navigate complex scenarios, infer missing information, and make intuitive leaps. Machines, on the other hand, rely heavily on explicit instructions and predefined rules. They struggle with ambiguity, context, and understanding subtle nuances that humans grasp instinctively.

Creativity, too, remains a uniquely human attribute. The ability to think outside the box, generate novel ideas, and engage in artistic pursuits is deeply ingrained in our cognitive abilities. While machines can generate content or art based on learned patterns, they lack the innate spark of human creativity, which often stems from a combination of emotions, experiences, and intuition.

Emotional intelligence, another vital aspect of human cognition, involves understanding and managing emotions, as well as perceiving and responding to the emotions of others. Machines, devoid of consciousness or subjective experiences, cannot truly comprehend emotions in the same way humans do. While they can analyse facial expressions or speech patterns to infer emotions, their understanding is limited to surface-level cues.

Moreover, the ethical implications of machine intelligence raise complex questions. As machines become more capable, issues such as job displacement, privacy, bias, and accountability come to the forefront. The responsibility of designing and deploying AI systems lies with humans, necessitating careful consideration of the potential societal impacts and ethical considerations involved.

Machine intelligence, fueled by advancements in artificial intelligence and machine learning, has transformed numerous industries and revolutionized the way we live and work. Machines are now capable of remarkable feats, from recognizing complex patterns in data to mastering complex games and autonomously driving vehicles. However, it is essential to understand that machine intelligence also has its limitations. In this exploration, we will delve into the capabilities and limitations of machine intelligence, highlighting the areas where machines excel and where human expertise remains indispensable.

One of the greatest strengths of machine intelligence lies in its ability to process vast amounts of data quickly and efficiently. Machines can analyse large datasets and identify patterns that may not be readily apparent to humans. This capability has led to significant advancements in fields such as image and speech recognition, natural language processing, and data analysis. Machine learning algorithms, inspired by the neural networks of the human brain, have proven highly effective in making predictions, optimizing outcomes, and automating tasks that were once time-consuming and labour-intensive.

Moreover, machines are not limited by human constraints such as fatigue, emotions, or biases. They can tirelessly perform repetitive tasks with consistent precision and accuracy, making them invaluable in industries such as manufacturing, logistics, and data management. Machine intelligence has also brought about significant advancements in medical diagnostics, where machines can analyse medical images and patient data to aid in the early detection of diseases and assist in treatment planning.

Another area where machine intelligence shines is in complex problem-solving. Through advanced algorithms and computational power, machines can explore vast solution spaces and identify optimal solutions in fields such as optimization, scheduling, and resource allocation. This capability has proven beneficial in areas such as supply chain management, transportation planning, and financial modelling. Machine intelligence has the potential to optimize processes and improve efficiency, leading to cost savings and better resource allocation.

Despite these impressive capabilities, machine intelligence does have its limitations. Machines lack the innate human qualities of common sense, intuition, and creativity. While they excel at processing data and recognizing patterns, they struggle with tasks that require abstract reasoning, contextual understanding, and deep domain expertise. Human intelligence, with its ability to grasp complex concepts, adapt to novel situations, and think critically, remains unparalleled.

Language understanding is another area where machines face significant challenges. While machine translation and natural language processing have made impressive strides, fully understanding and interpreting human language in all its nuances, idioms, and cultural contexts remains a complex problem. Machines often struggle with ambiguity, sarcasm, and implicit meanings, which can lead to misinterpretations and errors in communication. Human language is deeply ingrained with cultural, social, and emotional nuances that are challenging for machines to grasp fully.

Ethical considerations and biases are also important limitations to consider. Machine learning algorithms learn from training data, and if that data contains biases or discriminatory patterns, the machines may replicate and amplify those biases. This can lead to unfair outcomes, perpetuating societal inequalities and reinforcing existing biases. It is crucial to address these ethical concerns and develop transparent and accountable approaches to ensure that machine intelligence is used responsibly and ethically.

Another limitation of machine intelligence is its inability to truly comprehend the world beyond the data it is trained on. Machines lack the embodied experience that humans possess, which allows us to understand concepts through sensory perception and physical interactions with the environment. Machines rely solely on the data they are provided, making them susceptible to data limitations, biases, and unforeseen situations that fall outside their training scope.

Lastly, machines still struggle with tasks that require high-level perceptual and sensorimotor skills. While advances in robotics have allowed machines to perform physical tasks with increasing dexterity, they still lack the adaptability, agility, and finesse of human motor skills. Tasks that involve fine manipulation, navigating complex environments, and responding to unexpected changes remain challenging for machines.

In the next chapter, we will delve deeper into the ongoing debate between human and machine intelligence, examining the potential future scenarios and the implications for our society. By understanding the capabilities and limitations of both domains, we can shape a future that maximizes the benefits of AI while ensuring the preservation of our human values and dignity.

So, let us continue our exploration, venturing into the realm of human and machine intelligence, pondering the possibilities and reflecting on the challenges that lie ahead. Together, we will navigate this complex landscape and strive to strike a harmonious balance between the remarkable capabilities of machines and the essence of what it means to be human.

Chapter 4: Unleashing the Dynamic Force of Machines

In this chapter, we shift our focus to machines and their evolving capabilities. From early computing machines to the advent of artificial intelligence (AI), we will trace the development and progress of machine learning. We will explore the rise of neural networks, deep learning algorithms, and the potential implications they hold for emulating human intelligence.

The journey of machines towards emulating human intelligence can be traced back to the early days of computing. In the mid-20th century, pioneers such as Alan Turing and John von Neumann laid the foundation for modern computing and introduced the concept of machines that could simulate human thought processes.

The field of artificial intelligence gained significant momentum in the 1950s and 1960s with the development of the first AI programs. Early AI systems focused on rule-based expert systems, where explicit rules and logical reasoning were used to mimic human decision-making. These systems showed promise in limited domains, such as chess playing and theorem proving, but their rigid rule-based approach made it challenging to generalize to broader contexts.

In the 1980s and 1990s, machine learning emerged as a subfield of AI, aiming to develop algorithms that could learn from data and improve their performance over time. This shift marked a significant departure from the rule-based approach and paved the way for more flexible and adaptable systems.

One key breakthrough in machine learning was the development of neural networks. Inspired by the structure and function of the human brain, neural networks are computational models consisting of interconnected nodes, or artificial neurons, organized in layers. These networks can process and analyse data, detecting patterns and making predictions based on the learned relationships between input and output data.

Early neural networks faced challenges due to limited computing power and datasets. However, advancements in hardware and the availability of large-scale datasets in the 21st century ignited a revolution in the field. This progress, combined with sophisticated algorithms and improved training techniques, led to the rise of deep learning.

Deep learning refers to the training of neural networks with multiple layers, allowing for the extraction of hierarchical representations of data. This hierarchical approach enables deep learning algorithms to learn abstract features at different levels of complexity, leading to superior performance in tasks such as image and speech recognition, natural language processing, and even playing complex games.

One notable milestone in the development of machine intelligence was the victory of the deep learning-based AlphaGo system over the world champion Go player in 2016. Go, a complex and ancient board game, was considered a grand challenge for AI due to its vast number of possible moves and the difficulty of evaluating positions. The success of AlphaGo demonstrated the potential of deep learning algorithms to surpass human expertise in domains traditionally thought to be exclusive to human intelligence.

The capabilities of deep learning algorithms extend beyond game playing. They have proven instrumental in various fields, such as healthcare, finance, and autonomous driving. For example, deep learning algorithms can analyse medical images to assist in disease diagnosis, predict market trends based on financial data, and enable self-driving cars to perceive and navigate the world.

However, it is important to recognize that the power of machines, even with advanced deep learning algorithms, is still limited in certain aspects compared to human cognition. While machines excel in data processing and pattern recognition, they often struggle with common-sense reasoning, creativity, and adapting to new situations.

Common-sense reasoning, the ability to make logical deductions based on prior knowledge and understanding of the world, remains a significant challenge for machines. Human intelligence effortlessly integrates context, background knowledge, and intuition to navigate complex scenarios. Machines, on the other hand, typically rely on explicit instructions and predefined rules, limiting their ability to handle ambiguity and make intuitive leaps.

Creativity, another hallmark of human intelligence, continues to elude machines. While machines can generate content or art based on learned patterns, they lack the spontaneous and innovative thinking that stems from human emotions, experiences, and intuition. The ability to think outside the box, generate novel ideas, and engage in artistic endeavours remains a uniquely human trait.

Additionally, the ethical implications of unleashing the power of machines cannot be ignored. As machines become more capable, concerns arise regarding job displacement, privacy, bias, and accountability. The responsible development and deployment of AI systems require careful consideration of these ethical considerations and a commitment to ensuring that the benefits of machine intelligence are maximized while minimizing potential negative impacts.

In conclusion, the journey of machines towards emulating human intelligence has witnessed remarkable progress. The development of neural networks and the rise of deep learning algorithms have revolutionized fields such as image recognition, natural language processing, and autonomous systems. However, machines still fall short in several aspects compared to human cognition, such as common-sense reasoning and creativity. Understanding the capabilities and limitations of machine intelligence is crucial in shaping a future where machines and humans can coexist harmoniously, leveraging the strengths of both domains. In the next chapter, we will delve into the societal implications of machine intelligence and explore how we can navigate the complex landscape of human-machine interaction.

In today's world, machines are revolutionizing the way we live, work, and interact. From early computing machines to the latest advancements in artificial intelligence, machines have continuously evolved to harness immense power and potential. They can process vast amounts of data, learn from patterns, and make predictions with unprecedented accuracy. The power of machines lies in their ability to automate tasks, solve complex problems, and augment human capabilities.

The rise of machine learning has unlocked new realms of possibility. Neural networks and deep learning algorithms allow machines to analyze and interpret data, recognize patterns, and make informed decisions. This has far-reaching implications across various industries, from healthcare and finance to transportation and entertainment. Machines can process data at incredible speeds, uncover hidden insights, and help us navigate the complexities of our modern world.

However, with this power comes responsibility. As we unleash the potential of machines, it is essential to ensure that their use aligns with ethical considerations and respects human values. We must carefully address issues such as algorithmic bias, privacy, and accountability. By doing so, we can harness the power of machines to drive innovation, improve efficiency, and create a better future for humanity. The possibilities are immense, and by unleashing the power of machines in a responsible and ethical manner, we can unlock a new era of human-machine collaboration that transcends our current limitations.

Chapter 5: Exploring the Multifaceted Realm of Human-Machine Interaction

As machine intelligence continues to advance, the interaction between humans and machines becomes increasingly significant. In this chapter, we will explore the complex landscape of human-machine interaction, addressing the challenges, opportunities, and ethical considerations that arise when humans and machines collaborate.

One area of human-machine interaction that has gained considerable attention is human-robot interaction (HRI). Robots are being designed and deployed in various domains, including healthcare, manufacturing, and customer service. The goal is to create robots that can understand human intentions, communicate effectively, and collaborate seamlessly with their human counterparts.

Effective HRI requires machines to perceive and understand human cues, such as gestures, facial expressions, and speech. Natural language processing plays a crucial role in enabling machines to understand and respond to human commands and inquiries. Additionally, advances in computer vision allow machines to interpret visual information and interact with their environment in a more intuitive manner.

However, HRI is not limited to physical robots. Virtual assistants, such as Siri, Alexa, and Google Assistant, have become prevalent in our daily lives. These intelligent systems rely on natural language processing and machine learning algorithms to understand and respond to human queries and requests. The success of these virtual assistants lies in their ability to adapt to individual users' preferences and provide personalized experiences.

While the convenience and efficiency of human-machine interaction are evident, ethical considerations come into play. Privacy concerns arise when interacting with intelligent systems that collect and process personal data. Safeguarding user information and ensuring data protection are vital to maintain trust in the use of these technologies.

Another ethical concern in human-machine interaction is bias. AI systems learn from data, and if the data used for training contains biases, the systems may perpetuate or amplify those biases. This can result in discriminatory outcomes, reinforcing social inequalities. It is crucial to address bias in AI algorithms and ensure fairness and equity in human-machine interactions.

As machines become more capable, questions of responsibility and accountability emerge. Who is responsible if an AI system makes an incorrect decision or causes harm? Ensuring transparency and accountability in the design, development, and deployment of AI systems is essential. Clear guidelines, regulations, and ethical frameworks need to be established to govern the actions and decisions of intelligent machines.

Furthermore, there is a need to consider the potential impact of automation on the workforce. As machines become more capable of performing tasks traditionally done by humans, job displacement becomes a concern. However, history has shown that technological advancements often create new job opportunities and lead to the emergence of new industries. It is crucial to anticipate these changes and ensure adequate support and retraining programs are in place to mitigate the impact on affected individuals.

Beyond the challenges, human-machine interaction also presents significant opportunities. Collaborative systems, where humans and machines work together to solve complex problems, hold great potential. Machines can analyse vast amounts of data and provide insights that humans may overlook. Meanwhile, humans bring creativity, critical thinking, and domain expertise to the table, complementing the analytical capabilities of machines.

Machines have evolved from simple tools to complex and intelligent entities that are reshaping the way we live, work, and interact with the world. The power of machines lies in their ability to process vast amounts of data, recognize patterns, and make informed decisions. From self-driving cars to virtual assistants, machines have become integral parts of our daily lives, revolutionizing industries and transforming society as a whole. In this exploration, we will delve into the extraordinary capabilities of machines, their potential for innovation, and the ethical considerations that arise as we unleash their power.

One of the key drivers behind the power of machines is artificial intelligence (AI). AI is a field of computer science that aims to develop machines capable of intelligent behavior and decision-making. Machine learning, a subset of AI, enables machines to learn from data and improve their performance over time without explicit programming. By leveraging algorithms and statistical models, machines can detect patterns, make predictions, and automate tasks that were once considered exclusive to human intelligence.

The impact of machine learning and AI is visible across various domains. In healthcare, machines can analyze medical images and identify potential diseases or abnormalities with a high level of accuracy. This not only aids in early diagnosis but also enables doctors to provide targeted treatments. In finance, machines can analyze vast amounts of financial data in real-time, identifying trends, and making informed investment decisions. This has transformed the financial industry, making it more efficient and accessible.

Machine learning algorithms have also revolutionized the way we interact with technology. Natural language processing allows machines to understand and respond to human language, enabling the development of virtual assistants like Siri and Alexa. These assistants can perform tasks, answer questions, and even engage in meaningful conversations. Additionally, machine learning powers recommendation systems, personalized advertisements, and predictive algorithms that enhance user experiences across various online platforms.

The power of machines is further amplified by their ability to analyze big data. In today's digital age, enormous volumes of data are generated every second. Machines can process and extract valuable insights from this data, leading to improved decision-making and innovation. From social media data to sensor data collected from devices connected to the Internet of Things (IoT), machines can uncover patterns and correlations that humans may overlook. These insights have far-reaching implications in fields such as marketing, healthcare, urban planning, and climate science.

The convergence of machines and data has also paved the way for automation and increased productivity. Repetitive and mundane tasks that consume human time and effort can now be automated, freeing up valuable resources for more creative and strategic endeavors. Manufacturing processes, customer support, and logistics have all benefited from the power of machines. Automation not only increases efficiency but also reduces errors, resulting in higher quality outputs.

While the power of machines is undeniably transformative, it is crucial to address the ethical considerations that arise. As machines become more autonomous and capable of making decisions, questions of accountability, fairness, and transparency come to the forefront. The algorithms powering machines are not immune to biases present in the data they are trained on, leading to potential discrimination and unfairness. It is essential to ensure that machines are trained on diverse and unbiased data and that their decision-making processes are transparent and explainable.

The impact of machines on employment is also a topic of concern. As automation becomes more prevalent, certain jobs may become obsolete, leading to unemployment and societal disruptions. However, history has shown that technological advancements often lead to the creation of new industries and job opportunities. It is crucial to anticipate these shifts and invest in education and retraining programs to prepare the workforce for the changing landscape.

Privacy and security are additional ethical considerations when unleashing the power of machines. The vast amounts of data collected and processed by machines raise concerns about the protection of personal information and the potential for misuse.

The combination of human and machine intelligence, often referred to as augmented intelligence or intelligence amplification, has the potential to revolutionize fields such as healthcare, scientific research, and decision-making processes. By harnessing the strengths of both humans and machines, we can achieve outcomes that surpass what either could achieve alone.

In conclusion, human-machine interaction is a multidimensional and dynamic field that raises both challenges and opportunities. As machines become increasingly integrated into our lives, it is essential to navigate this complex landscape with careful consideration of ethical, social, and economic implications. By fostering responsible development, establishing ethical frameworks, and embracing collaboration between humans and machines, we can shape a future where intelligent technologies enhance human capabilities and improve the well-being of society as a whole.

Chapter 6: Harmonizing Machine Intelligence and Human Intelligence

In this chapter, we delve into the heart of the debate: the comparison between machine intelligence and human intelligence. The question of whether machines can replicate or exceed human cognitive abilities has intrigued researchers, philosophers, and the general public alike. Let us explore various perspectives on this topic, considering arguments for and against the idea that machines can truly emulate the complexity of human intelligence.

One of the key areas where humans have long been considered superior to machines is creativity. The ability to think outside the box, generate novel ideas, and engage in artistic endeavours has been regarded as a hallmark of human intelligence. While machines have shown remarkable capabilities in generating content based on learned patterns, there is a fundamental difference between the replication of patterns and the creation of truly original and innovative ideas.

Human creativity often stems from a combination of emotions, experiences, and intuition. It is deeply intertwined with our consciousness and subjective experiences. Machines, on the other hand, lack consciousness and subjective experiences, making it difficult for them to replicate the depth and richness of human creativity. While machines can generate content that may appear creative, it is ultimately based on existing patterns and algorithms, lacking the spontaneous and original spark of human imagination.

Another aspect of human intelligence that has posed a challenge for machines is emotional intelligence. Emotional intelligence involves understanding and managing emotions, as well as perceiving and responding to the emotions of others. It is a complex and multifaceted trait that combines cognitive processes with empathy and social awareness.

Machines, by their very nature, lack consciousness and subjective experiences, which are integral to emotional intelligence. While they can analyse facial expressions, speech patterns, and other cues to infer emotions, their understanding remains limited to surface-level observations. Machines may be able to simulate emotional responses or provide appropriate feedback in certain situations, but they lack the deep emotional understanding and empathy that humans possess.

Consciousness itself is a deeply philosophical and debated topic. Human consciousness encompasses our subjective experiences, self-awareness, and the ability to introspect. It is a complex phenomenon that is still not fully understood. While machines can exhibit intelligent behaviour, they do not possess subjective consciousness. They lack the qualia—the subjective aspects of experience that make consciousness uniquely human.

Moreover, the human brain operates in a highly parallel and interconnected manner, enabling the seamless integration of sensory information, emotions, and reasoning processes. Machines, on the other hand, typically operate in a sequential and deterministic manner. While advances in neural networks have allowed for more parallel processing, machines still fall short in replicating the intricate and holistic nature of human cognition.

However, it is important to acknowledge the remarkable progress machines have made in emulating certain aspects of human intelligence. They excel in data processing, pattern recognition, and decision-making based on learned patterns. Machine learning algorithms can analyse vast amounts of data, detect subtle patterns, and make predictions with high accuracy. This has led to breakthroughs in fields such as image recognition, natural language processing, and even autonomous systems.

Furthermore, machines have surpassed human performance in specific tasks, such as playing chess, Go, and other games. These achievements demonstrate the remarkable analytical capabilities of machines and their ability to process information at incredible speeds.

The realms of machine intelligence and human intelligence have long been subjects of intrigue and comparison. Both possess unique capabilities, but their underlying mechanisms and potential applications differ significantly. Machine intelligence, powered by algorithms and artificial intelligence, has made remarkable strides in recent years, while human intelligence remains the pinnacle of cognitive abilities. In this exploration, we will delve into the similarities, differences, and potential synergies between machine intelligence and human intelligence, examining their respective strengths, limitations, and the implications they hold for the future.

Machine intelligence, often referred to as artificial intelligence (AI), encompasses the ability of machines to perform tasks that typically require human intelligence. Through algorithms and data processing, machines can analyze vast amounts of information, recognize patterns, make predictions, and automate complex processes. Machine learning, a subset of AI, allows machines to improve their performance over time by learning from data without explicit programming. This has revolutionized industries such as healthcare, finance, transportation, and entertainment, enabling unprecedented advancements and efficiency.

One of the primary advantages of machine intelligence is its ability to process and analyze large amounts of data quickly and accurately. Machines excel at tasks involving repetitive calculations, data mining, and pattern recognition. In areas such as image and speech recognition, natural language processing, and recommendation systems, machines have surpassed human capabilities, achieving levels of accuracy and speed that were previously unimaginable. Moreover, machines can tirelessly perform tasks without fatigue or the limitations of human attention span.

Human intelligence, on the other hand, encompasses a broad range of cognitive abilities that go beyond pattern recognition and data processing. It includes perception, creativity, emotional intelligence, critical thinking, and abstract reasoning. Human intelligence is rooted in the brain's intricate neural networks, which enable complex information processing, the integration of sensory input, and the generation of novel ideas. Human intelligence is also deeply connected to our ability to learn from experience, adapt to new situations, and apply knowledge creatively.

One of the distinctive qualities of human intelligence is our capacity for subjective experiences and consciousness. While machines can simulate and mimic human-like behaviors, they lack true consciousness and self-awareness. Human intelligence encompasses the rich tapestry of emotions, the ability to reflect on oneself and others, and the capacity to derive meaning and purpose from our experiences. These aspects of human intelligence give rise to empathy, moral reasoning, and social interactions, which play crucial roles in our personal and collective lives.

Despite the remarkable advancements in machine intelligence, there are inherent limitations that distinguish it from human intelligence. Machines are highly specialized and excel in specific domains, but they struggle with tasks that humans find effortless. Common-sense reasoning, contextual understanding, and the ability to navigate complex social dynamics are areas where machines still fall short. Additionally, machines lack the ability to generalize knowledge across domains or transfer learning from one task to another as effectively as humans can.

The combination of human intelligence and machine intelligence holds tremendous potential for synergistic collaboration. Human expertise, creativity, and intuition can guide the development of intelligent machines, ensuring they align with human values and serve human needs. Machines, in turn, can augment human intelligence, enabling us to process information more efficiently, make better-informed decisions, and address complex challenges. Human-machine collaboration has the potential to transform industries such as healthcare, scientific research, education, and many more.

Ethical considerations play a crucial role in the development and deployment of machine intelligence. As machines become increasingly capable, questions arise about privacy, security, and the potential impact on employment and societal structures. It is imperative to establish ethical frameworks and guidelines to ensure that machine intelligence is harnessed responsibly, with a focus on benefiting humanity as a whole. Transparency, accountability, and inclusivity should guide the development of machine intelligence systems to minimize potential biases and ensure fair and equitable outcomes.

It is also important to note that the goal of machine intelligence is not necessarily to replicate human intelligence entirely. Machines offer unique capabilities that complement human abilities. They can process and analyse vast amounts of data quickly and accurately, providing valuable insights and assisting humans in decision-making processes. The collaboration between humans and machines, often referred to as symbiotic intelligence, holds great potential in solving complex problems and advancing various fields.

However, despite the impressive achievements of machines, there are fundamental differences between machine intelligence and human intelligence. Human cognition is deeply intertwined with our consciousness, emotions, experiences, and the richness of our subjective existence. It is the product of billions of years of evolution and shaped by complex biological and environmental factors.

In conclusion, while machines have made remarkable strides in emulating certain aspects of human intelligence, they still fall short in replicating the depth, richness, and complexity of human cognition. The abilities of creativity, emotional intelligence, consciousness, and the holistic nature of human cognition remain elusive for machines. However, the goal should not be to replicate human intelligence entirely but rather to leverage the unique strengths of both humans and machines to create a future where intelligent technologies enhance human capabilities and improve the well-being of society as a whole.

Chapter 7: The Evolving Landscape of Intelligence: Embracing Synergy and Coexistence

As we ponder the comparison between machine intelligence and human intelligence, it is important to shift our focus towards the future and explore the potential for synergy and coexistence between humans and machines. Rather than framing it as a competition, we can envision a future where intelligent machines and human beings work together, leveraging their respective strengths to tackle complex challenges and improve the human experience.

One area where the collaboration between humans and machines shows great promise is in the field of healthcare. Intelligent systems can analyse vast amounts of patient data, assist in disease diagnosis, and suggest personalized treatment plans. Machines can process medical images, identify anomalies, and provide doctors with valuable insights, leading to more accurate and timely diagnoses. The combination of human medical expertise and machine intelligence has the potential to revolutionize healthcare, improving patient outcomes and reducing medical errors.

In scientific research, machines can help analyse large datasets, simulate complex phenomena, and identify patterns that might elude human researchers. By automating repetitive tasks and data analysis, machines free up human researchers to focus on higher-level thinking, hypothesis generation, and experimental design. This collaborative approach can accelerate scientific discoveries and lead to breakthroughs in fields such as genomics, drug discovery, and climate modelling.

Another domain where human-machine collaboration is gaining traction is in the realm of creativity and artistic expression. Machines can assist artists in generating ideas, exploring new styles, and even producing art based on learned patterns. This collaboration can expand the boundaries of human creativity, pushing the limits of what is possible and inspiring new artistic endeavours. Machines can act as creative partners, providing suggestions, enhancing artistic techniques, and fostering innovation in the creative process.

In the realm of decision-making, machines can augment human capabilities by processing vast amounts of data, analysing complex scenarios, and providing evidence-based recommendations. From business strategies to policy-making, the combination of human judgment and machine intelligence can lead to more informed and effective decision-making processes. Machines can help identify potential risks, predict outcomes, and guide humans towards more favourable outcomes.

However, as we embrace the potential of human-machine collaboration, it is crucial to address the ethical considerations that arise. Transparency, fairness, and accountability are essential in ensuring that the integration of machines into various domains is done responsibly. Safeguards must be in place to prevent biases, protect privacy, and ensure that the power of machine intelligence is wielded for the benefit of society as a whole.

Education and training will play a vital role in preparing individuals for a future where machines are integrated into various aspects of our lives. Developing skills that complement and leverage machine intelligence, such as critical thinking, creativity, emotional intelligence, and ethical reasoning, will be crucial. Education systems must adapt to this changing landscape, equipping individuals with the knowledge and skills necessary to thrive in a world where human-machine collaboration is the norm.

In conclusion, the future of intelligence lies in synergy and coexistence between humans and machines. Rather than viewing it as a competition, we can harness the unique strengths of both domains to create a future that is more intelligent, innovative, and compassionate.

The integration of machine intelligence into various fields has the potential to enhance human capabilities,

The future holds great promise and challenges as the realms of human intelligence and machine intelligence converge. The synergy and coexistence of these two forms of intelligence will shape our world in unprecedented ways, impacting every aspect of society, from healthcare and transportation to education and entertainment. In this exploration, we will delve into the potential future scenarios where human and machine intelligence intersect, examining the opportunities, risks, and the implications they hold for our collective future.

The journey towards the future of intelligence is characterized by a symbiotic relationship between human intelligence and machine intelligence. While machines have made remarkable strides in replicating human-like behaviors and cognitive abilities, they still lack the depth and complexity of human intelligence. Conversely, humans possess inherent qualities such as creativity, empathy, and abstract reasoning that are yet to be fully replicated in machines. Therefore, the future lies not in a competition between the two forms of intelligence, but in their collaboration and complementarity.

One of the most promising aspects of the future of intelligence lies in human-machine collaboration. Humans and machines can leverage each other's strengths to achieve outcomes that surpass what either can accomplish alone. Machines excel at data processing, pattern recognition, and automation, while humans bring unique qualities such as intuition, critical thinking, and emotional intelligence to the table. By working together, humans and machines can tackle complex problems, make better-informed decisions, and drive innovation across industries.

Education is one area where the synergy between human and machine intelligence holds significant potential. Intelligent tutoring systems and adaptive learning platforms can personalize education experiences, tailoring content to individual needs and learning styles. Machines can assist teachers by automating administrative tasks, providing real-time feedback to students, and analyzing vast amounts of data to identify trends and insights. This collaborative approach enhances the learning process, allowing humans to focus on fostering creativity, critical thinking, and social skills.

Healthcare is another domain where the future of intelligence promises transformative advancements. Machine learning algorithms can analyze vast amounts of patient data, enabling early detection of diseases, more accurate diagnoses, and personalized treatment plans. Robots and automated systems can assist healthcare professionals in surgical procedures, monitoring patients, and providing care to individuals with limited mobility. Human healthcare providers, with their expertise and empathy, can focus on building relationships with patients, providing emotional support, and making complex medical decisions.

The future of work will undoubtedly be shaped by the integration of human and machine intelligence. While some jobs may be automated, new opportunities will emerge that require a hybrid skill set combining technical knowledge with social and emotional intelligence. Machines can handle routine and repetitive tasks, freeing up humans to engage in more creative and value-driven work. Collaboration between humans and machines in fields such as data analysis, design, research, and innovation will lead to new possibilities and economic growth.

Ethical considerations will play a crucial role in navigating the future of intelligence. As machines become increasingly capable, questions of privacy, security, bias, and the impact on employment and social structures arise. It is essential to establish ethical frameworks, regulations, and transparency to ensure the responsible development and deployment of intelligent systems. Emphasizing human values, diversity, and inclusivity in the design and implementation of AI systems will help mitigate potential risks and ensure fair and equitable outcomes.

The future of intelligence also raises philosophical and existential questions. As machines become more advanced, the boundaries between human and machine intelligence may become blurred. This raises questions about the nature of consciousness, free will, and what it means to be human. Exploring these questions and engaging in interdisciplinary discussions will be crucial to shape the future of intelligence in a way that aligns with our values and preserves the essence of human existence.

improve decision-making, advance scientific research, and revolutionize industries. By embracing responsible development, fostering collaboration, and addressing ethical considerations, we can shape a future where humans and machines work together to tackle grand challenges and create a more prosperous and inclusive world.

The future of intelligence lies in the synergy and coexistence of human and machine minds. As we continue to advance in technology and artificial intelligence, the boundaries between human and machine intelligence become increasingly blurred. Rather than seeing this as a competition, the true potential lies in harnessing the strengths of both. Human creativity, empathy, and critical thinking combined with machine speed, efficiency, and data processing capabilities can unlock new frontiers of innovation. It is through collaboration, understanding, and responsible development that we can shape a future where human and machine intelligences thrive in harmony, driving progress and addressing complex challenges.

Chapter 8: Synergy through Collaboration

In this chapter, we shift our perspective from the comparison between human intelligence and machine intelligence to the concept of synergy and collaboration. Rather than viewing humans and machines as adversaries, we explore the potential for harmonious collaboration, where the unique strengths of each are combined to drive innovation, solve complex problems, and enhance the human experience.

One of the domains where human-machine collaboration has already made significant strides is in the field of medicine. Intelligent systems, such as IBM's Watson, have been employed to assist doctors in diagnosing and treating patients. These systems can analyse vast amounts of medical literature, patient data, and clinical guidelines to provide evidence-based recommendations to healthcare professionals. By leveraging machine intelligence, doctors can make more informed decisions, leading to improved patient outcomes and more personalized healthcare.

In the realm of scientific research, human-machine collaboration has also proven to be fruitful. For example, in the field of astronomy, machine learning algorithms have been employed to analyse massive amounts of data from telescopes and satellites. These algorithms can identify patterns, detect celestial objects, and classify astronomical phenomena with incredible precision. By partnering with intelligent machines, astronomers can accelerate the process of discovery and gain deeper insights into the universe.

In the creative realm, human-machine collaboration has opened up new avenues for artistic expression. Artists can now employ machine learning algorithms and generative models to explore new artistic styles, generate unique compositions, and push the boundaries of creativity. The algorithms can learn from existing artistic works and assist artists in generating novel ideas or even autonomously producing art. This collaboration between human creativity and machine intelligence leads to new artistic possibilities and sparks innovative approaches to artistic expression.

In business and industry, human-machine collaboration has the potential to revolutionize various processes. Intelligent systems can assist in data analysis, forecasting, and decision-making. For instance, in the financial sector, machine learning algorithms can analyse market trends, historical data, and news events to generate insights and predictions for investment decisions. The combination of human expertise and machine intelligence leads to more informed and effective strategies, reducing risks and maximizing opportunities.

In the realm of transportation, the collaboration between humans and machines has already started to shape the future. Self-driving cars, for example, rely on a combination of sensors, machine learning algorithms, and human oversight to navigate roads safely. While machines handle the tasks of perception and control, human drivers are still responsible for monitoring and taking over in complex situations. This collaboration aims to enhance road safety, optimize traffic flow, and reduce human error.

While these examples illustrate the potential of human-machine collaboration, it is important to address the challenges that come with it. Ensuring transparency, fairness, and accountability in the decision-making processes of intelligent machines is crucial. Ethical considerations such as bias, privacy, and security must be carefully addressed to maintain trust and ensure that the collaboration between humans and machines is beneficial for all.

Education and training play a vital role in preparing individuals for a future where collaboration with machines is integral. The focus should be on developing skills that complement and leverage machine intelligence, such as critical thinking, creativity, adaptability, and emotional intelligence. Education systems must adapt to equip individuals with the necessary knowledge and skills to thrive in a world where human-machine collaboration is the norm.

Synergy and collaboration are two powerful concepts that have the potential to transform individuals, organizations, and societies as a whole. When harnessed effectively, they can lead to remarkable achievements, innovation, and the collective pursuit of common goals. In this exploration, we will delve into the essence of synergy and collaboration, examining their significance, benefits, and the ways in which they can shape our present and future.

Synergy is the harmonious interaction of multiple elements, entities, or individuals, resulting in a combined effect that exceeds the sum of their individual contributions. It is the art of bringing together diverse perspectives, skills, and resources to create something greater than what could be achieved in isolation. Synergy is not simply the result of collaboration, but rather the result of collaboration that transcends individual efforts and leads to a whole that is greater than the sum of its parts.

Collaboration, on the other hand, is the process of working together towards a common goal. It involves individuals or groups pooling their knowledge, expertise, and resources, leveraging their collective strengths to achieve shared objectives. Collaboration is fueled by effective communication, trust, and a shared vision. It requires individuals to set aside personal agendas and ego, embracing a mindset of openness, cooperation, and mutual respect.

The benefits of synergy and collaboration are manifold. By combining diverse perspectives and expertise, synergy enables us to tap into a broader range of ideas and possibilities. It fosters creativity and innovation, as different viewpoints and approaches converge to generate novel solutions and insights. Collaboration promotes learning and growth, as individuals learn from one another, share knowledge and experiences, and collectively expand their capabilities. It also fosters a sense of belonging and collective ownership, creating a supportive and inclusive environment.

Synergy and collaboration have profound implications for various domains, including business, science, education, and social change. In the business world, collaboration among teams and departments can enhance productivity, efficiency, and problem-solving. By leveraging the collective intelligence and skills of employees, organizations can drive innovation, adapt to changing markets, and gain a competitive edge. Collaborative partnerships between businesses and other stakeholders, such as customers, suppliers, and communities, can also lead to mutual benefits and sustainable growth.

In scientific research, collaboration plays a crucial role in advancing knowledge and solving complex problems. Collaborative research efforts bring together experts from different disciplines, enabling cross-pollination of ideas and methodologies. By sharing resources, data, and insights, scientists can accelerate discoveries, tackle grand challenges, and address pressing societal issues. Collaborative networks and institutions foster a culture of knowledge exchange, encouraging the development of breakthrough innovations and solutions.

In the realm of education, collaboration is fundamental to creating engaging and effective learning environments. Collaborative learning approaches, such as group projects, discussions, and peer-to-peer interactions, promote active participation, critical thinking, and social skills. Students learn from one another, develop a deeper understanding of the subject matter, and acquire valuable teamwork and communication skills. Collaboration between educators, policymakers, and communities can also drive educational reforms and improve outcomes for learners.

On a broader scale, collaboration is essential for driving social change and addressing global challenges. Collaborative initiatives involving governments, non-governmental organizations, businesses, and communities can tackle issues such as poverty, climate change, and inequality. By aligning efforts, sharing resources, and coordinating actions, collaborative endeavors have the potential to create lasting impact and foster sustainable development. Collaboration empowers individuals and communities to collectively address complex problems that no single entity could solve alone.

While synergy and collaboration offer immense potential, they also come with challenges. Collaboration requires effective communication, active listening, and conflict resolution skills. It necessitates finding common ground, managing differing viewpoints, and navigating power dynamics. Building trust and fostering a culture of collaboration takes time and effort.

In conclusion, the concept of synergy and collaboration between humans and machines opens up new possibilities and potential for innovation. By combining the strengths of human intelligence, such as creativity, empathy, and ethical reasoning, with the analytical power and processing capabilities of machine intelligence, we can tackle complex problems and drive progress in various domains. As we navigate this collaboration, it is important to address ethical considerations, invest in education and training, and embrace a future where humans and machines work together harmoniously, ushering in a new era of technological advancement and human well-being.

Synergy and collaboration between humans and machines hold the key to unlocking new possibilities. By harnessing the unique strengths of both, we can achieve remarkable outcomes that surpass what either can accomplish alone. The fusion of human creativity, intuition, and emotional intelligence with the computational power and precision of machines can revolutionize fields such as healthcare, research, and creative endeavors. Together, humans and machines can transcend limitations, tackle complex challenges, and pave the way for a future where innovation knows no bounds. Synergy and collaboration form the foundation for a harmonious partnership that propels us towards a world of endless potential.

Chapter 9: Unleashing the Transformative Power: The Social Impact of Human-Machine Collaboration

In this chapter, we delve into the social impact of human-machine collaboration, examining both the potential benefits and challenges that arise as humans and machines work together in various domains. We explore the implications for employment, inequality, and the overall well-being of individuals and society. Additionally, we discuss the importance of fostering inclusivity and ethical considerations to ensure that the benefits of collaboration are distributed equitably.

One of the primary concerns surrounding human-machine collaboration is its impact on employment. As machines become increasingly capable of performing tasks traditionally carried out by humans, there is a legitimate fear of job displacement. However, history has shown that while certain jobs may be automated, new opportunities for employment often arise. Machines can handle repetitive and mundane tasks, freeing up human workers to focus on higher-level responsibilities that require creativity, critical thinking, and emotional intelligence.

Moreover, human-machine collaboration can lead to the creation of entirely new job roles and industries. As machines augment human capabilities, there is a growing need for individuals who can effectively collaborate with intelligent systems, interpret their outputs, and make informed decisions based on their recommendations. This shift in the nature of work calls for ongoing education and training initiatives to ensure that individuals are equipped with the skills required to thrive in this changing landscape.

Another aspect to consider is the potential for inequality resulting from human-machine collaboration. If access to intelligent technologies and the necessary skills to collaborate with machines are limited to certain segments of the population, a digital divide may emerge, exacerbating existing social and economic disparities. Efforts must be made to ensure that the benefits of collaboration are accessible to all and that individuals from diverse backgrounds have the opportunity to participate and contribute.

Inclusivity and diversity in the development and deployment of intelligent technologies are essential to prevent biases and ensure equitable outcomes. It is crucial to address issues of algorithmic bias and discriminatory practices that may arise from relying solely on machine intelligence. Human oversight and intervention are necessary to ensure that the decisions made by machines align with ethical standards and do not perpetuate existing biases or discrimination.

Additionally, considerations of privacy and data protection become paramount as human-machine collaboration becomes more prevalent. Intelligent systems rely on vast amounts of data to learn and make informed decisions. It is essential to establish robust regulations and frameworks to safeguard individuals' privacy and prevent the misuse of personal data. Transparency and accountability in the collection, storage, and use of data are crucial to maintaining trust and ensuring that collaboration is conducted ethically.

Furthermore, as human-machine collaboration becomes more integrated into society, it is vital to consider the psychological and social implications. The reliance on machines for decision-making may impact individuals' sense of autonomy and agency. Balancing the benefits of efficiency and accuracy with the need for human control and involvement is crucial to preserve individuals' well-being and maintain a sense of dignity and purpose.

In conclusion, human-machine collaboration holds immense potential for driving innovation, solving complex problems, and enhancing the human experience. However, it is crucial to address the social impact of collaboration to ensure that the benefits are widespread and that individuals from all walks of life have the opportunity to participate and benefit. By fostering inclusivity, addressing inequalities, and upholding ethical standards, we can navigate the evolving landscape of human-machine collaboration in a way that promotes social well-being, empowers individuals, and creates a more equitable and prosperous future.

Human-machine collaboration is revolutionizing the way we live, work, and interact with technology. As machines become increasingly capable and intelligent, their integration into various aspects of society has profound social implications. In this exploration, we will delve into the social impact of human-machine collaboration, examining its benefits, challenges, and the transformations it brings to our collective future.

One of the primary social benefits of human-machine collaboration lies in its potential to enhance productivity and efficiency. Machines excel at automating repetitive tasks, data analysis, and complex calculations, freeing up human time and energy for more creative and strategic endeavors. By collaborating with machines, humans can leverage their unique cognitive abilities, intuition, and decision-making skills, while machines provide the computational power and precision necessary for processing vast amounts of data. This partnership enables individuals and organizations to achieve more in less time, driving economic growth and innovation.

Another significant social impact of human-machine collaboration is its potential to address societal challenges and improve quality of life. Collaborative efforts between humans and machines have the power to tackle complex problems such as climate change, healthcare, and poverty. For example, machine learning algorithms can analyze environmental data to identify patterns and propose sustainable solutions. In healthcare, intelligent systems can assist doctors in diagnosis and treatment planning, improving patient outcomes. By combining human expertise with machine capabilities, we can collectively work towards a more sustainable, equitable, and healthier future.

Human-machine collaboration also has the potential to bridge societal divides and promote inclusivity. Intelligent technologies can assist individuals with disabilities, empowering them to engage more fully in social, educational, and professional spheres. Accessibility features, such as speech recognition and visual aids, enable people with disabilities to navigate digital interfaces and communicate effectively. Collaborative robots and exoskeletons assist individuals with mobility impairments, enhancing their independence and participation in society. By leveraging technology, we can create a more inclusive and accessible world for all.

However, the social impact of human-machine collaboration is not without its challenges. One key concern is the potential displacement of jobs and changes in the labor market. As automation and artificial intelligence advance, some tasks traditionally performed by humans may be taken over by machines. This transformation can lead to job losses and require individuals to adapt their skills to remain relevant in the workforce. It is essential for society to address these challenges through education, retraining programs, and the creation of new job opportunities that leverage the unique capabilities of humans in collaboration with machines.

Ethical considerations also play a crucial role in human-machine collaboration. As machines become more intelligent, questions of responsibility, accountability, and decision-making authority arise. It is essential to establish ethical frameworks and regulations that govern the development and deployment of intelligent systems. Transparency, explainability, and fairness should guide the design of algorithms and the collection and use of data. Additionally, ensuring that the benefits of human-machine collaboration are distributed equitably and that potential biases are identified and mitigated are important social considerations.

The social impact of human-machine collaboration extends to our daily lives and interactions. Intelligent assistants and chatbots are becoming increasingly prevalent in customer service, providing quick and personalized support. Social media platforms use machine learning algorithms to curate content and recommend connections, shaping our online experiences and influencing our perspectives. Collaborative filtering algorithms suggest personalized recommendations for movies, music, and products, influencing our consumption choices. These examples highlight how human-machine collaboration shapes our digital experiences and raises questions about privacy, algorithmic biases, and the power of recommendation systems.

The social impact of human-machine collaboration is profound and far-reaching. As intelligent machines become integrated into various aspects of our lives, they have the potential to transform industries, reshape employment landscapes, and impact societal dynamics. The adoption of automation and artificial intelligence technologies has the capacity to increase productivity and efficiency, leading to economic growth and job creation.

However, it also raises concerns about job displacement and inequality. It is crucial to ensure that the benefits of human-machine collaboration are distributed equitably and that individuals have access to the necessary skills and opportunities to adapt to the changing work environment. Moreover, the ethical implications of human-machine collaboration must be carefully considered. Issues such as privacy, algorithmic bias, and transparency need to be addressed to protect individual rights and uphold ethical standards. By fostering inclusive access, providing support for affected individuals, and developing responsible policies, we can harness the potential of human-machine collaboration to create a society that is more prosperous, equitable, and resilient.

Chapter 10: Ethical Reflections

In this chapter, we delve into the ethical considerations that arise in the context of artificial intelligence and machine learning. As machines become more intelligent and capable, it is crucial to address the ethical challenges that emerge to ensure that the use of these technologies aligns with our values and respects human rights.

One of the primary ethical concerns in the age of machine intelligence is privacy. Intelligent systems rely on vast amounts of data to learn and make informed decisions. The collection, storage, and use of personal data raise questions about consent, transparency, and the potential for misuse. It is essential to establish robust regulations and frameworks that prioritize the privacy and security of individuals' data, providing individuals with control over their personal information and ensuring that it is used responsibly and ethically.

Another ethical challenge is the presence of bias in algorithms. Machine learning algorithms learn from historical data, and if that data contains biases, the algorithms can perpetuate and even amplify those biases in their decision-making processes. This can lead to discriminatory outcomes in areas such as hiring, lending, and criminal justice. Addressing algorithmic bias requires careful attention to data collection, algorithm design, and ongoing monitoring and evaluation to ensure fairness and mitigate bias as much as possible.

Job displacement is also an ethical concern associated with the advancement of machine intelligence. As machines automate certain tasks, there is a risk of significant job losses in certain sectors. It is essential to consider the social and economic implications of these changes and work towards strategies that support the affected individuals, such as retraining programs, job transitions, and creating new opportunities that leverage human skills and creativity.

Ethics, the study of moral principles and values, plays a crucial role in guiding our actions, decisions, and behaviors. In a rapidly advancing world where technology, science, and societal dynamics constantly evolve, ethical considerations become even more critical. They help us navigate the complexities of our choices and ensure that we uphold principles such as fairness, justice, and respect for all. In this exploration, we will delve into the realm of ethical considerations, examining their significance, challenges, and the ways in which they shape our personal and collective lives.

Ethical considerations are at the heart of decision-making processes, influencing our behaviors and determining the consequences of our actions. They help us navigate ethical dilemmas, where there may be conflicting values or choices that impact individuals, communities, or the environment. Ethical considerations provide a framework for evaluating the moral implications of our decisions and guide us towards choices that align with our values and societal norms.

In today's interconnected world, ethical considerations have expanded beyond individual actions to encompass broader contexts such as business practices, technological developments, healthcare, and environmental stewardship. Ethical dilemmas arise in fields such as artificial intelligence, genetic engineering, privacy rights, and social justice. The consequences of our choices extend beyond immediate outcomes, impacting future generations and the well-being of our planet.

One of the fundamental ethical principles is respect for autonomy, recognizing and honoring an individual's right to make their own decisions and have control over their lives. This principle is particularly significant in the context of healthcare, where informed consent, patient confidentiality, and respect for personal choices are essential. Ethical considerations also involve justice, ensuring fairness and equitable distribution of resources, opportunities, and benefits. This principle underpins debates on income inequality, social welfare, and access to education and healthcare.

Ethical considerations also extend to the responsible use of technology and the development of artificial intelligence (AI). As AI becomes increasingly advanced and pervasive, questions arise regarding privacy, bias, and the potential impact on employment and societal structures. Ethical frameworks are needed to guide the development and deployment of AI systems, ensuring transparency, accountability, and the prevention of harm. Issues such as algorithmic fairness, data privacy, and the ethical implications of autonomous systems require careful evaluation and ongoing discourse.

Environmental ethics is another crucial aspect of ethical considerations. As we face pressing challenges such as climate change, deforestation, and resource depletion, ethical choices related to sustainability and environmental preservation become paramount. The long-term consequences of our actions on the planet and future generations demand ethical reflection and responsible decision-making. Ethical considerations guide us towards sustainable practices, conservation efforts, and the promotion of environmental justice.

Navigating ethical considerations is not without its challenges. In complex situations, there may be competing ethical principles or values that require careful analysis and prioritization. Different cultures and societies may have varying ethical frameworks, further complicating the process. Ethical considerations also require us to grapple with uncertainty and anticipate the potential consequences of our choices. Balancing short-term interests with long-term sustainability and societal well-being can be a delicate task.

Moreover, ethical considerations evolve as our knowledge, technology, and societal norms evolve. Ethical frameworks must be adaptable and responsive to changing contexts and new challenges. Ethical discourse, interdisciplinary dialogue, and engagement with diverse perspectives are essential for addressing emerging ethical issues and ensuring inclusivity in decision-making processes.

Ethical considerations are not merely intellectual exercises; they have tangible impacts on individuals, communities, and the world at large. They shape our identities, influence our relationships, and contribute to the fabric of our societies. By consciously engaging with ethical considerations, we can foster a culture of responsibility, empathy, and accountability. Ethical leadership, both at the individual and institutional levels, is crucial for shaping a more just, sustainable, and compassionate world.

The reliance on machines for decision-making raises concerns about accountability and responsibility. When machines are entrusted with critical decisions in areas such as healthcare, finance, and law enforcement, it becomes crucial to establish clear lines of responsibility and mechanisms for human oversight. Human accountability is necessary to ensure that decisions made by machines align with ethical standards, and to address the potential for unintended consequences or errors that may arise from relying solely on automated systems.

Transparency is another key ethical consideration. As intelligent systems make decisions that impact individuals' lives, it is important to provide transparency regarding the factors and criteria used in the decision-making process. Individuals should have the ability to understand how and why decisions are made, and to seek recourse or challenge decisions when necessary. Transparent systems also enable experts and regulators to assess the fairness and ethical implications of machine-driven decisions.

Additionally, as machines become more autonomous, there is a need to consider the potential risks associated with delegating too much decision-making power to machines. The concept of "machine ethics" arises, questioning whether machines can possess moral agency and make ethical judgments. It is crucial to strike a balance between the capabilities and limitations of machines and the involvement of human values and judgment to ensure that ethical considerations are not overlooked or compromised.

In conclusion, the advancement of machine intelligence brings forth ethical challenges that require careful consideration. Privacy, algorithmic bias, job displacement, accountability, transparency, and the risks associated with autonomous decision-making are among the key concerns. By proactively addressing these ethical considerations through robust regulations, responsible development practices, and ongoing dialogue, we can foster the ethical use of machine intelligence and ensure that it aligns with our values, respects human rights, and contributes to the betterment of society as a whole.

Chapter 11: The Evolution of Human-Machine Collaboration: Unveiling a New Era of Interaction

In this final chapter, we explore the future of human-machine interaction and the potential impact it may have on our society, economy, and daily lives. We consider emerging technologies, societal attitudes, and the ongoing evolution of human-machine collaboration. From augmented reality and brain-computer interfaces to ethical frameworks and policy development, we delve into the possibilities that lie ahead.

One of the key areas of development in the future of human-machine interaction is augmented reality (AR). AR technology allows us to overlay digital information and virtual objects onto the real world, enhancing our perception and interaction with our surroundings. This has the potential to revolutionize fields such as education, healthcare, and entertainment. Imagine students exploring virtual environments, doctors visualizing medical data in real-time, and users engaging in immersive gaming experiences. As AR technology advances, it will further blur the line between the physical and digital realms, shaping how we learn, work, and entertain ourselves.

Brain-computer interfaces (BCIs) represent another exciting frontier in human-machine interaction. BCIs enable direct communication between the brain and external devices, allowing individuals to control technology with their thoughts. This technology holds great promise for individuals with disabilities, offering them new means of mobility, communication, and independence. Additionally, BCIs have the potential to enhance cognitive abilities, enabling individuals to augment their memory, attention, and learning capacity. However, the ethical implications of BCIs, such as privacy and potential misuse, must be carefully considered and addressed to ensure their responsible development and use.

Societal attitudes towards human-machine interaction will also play a significant role in shaping the future. As intelligent machines become more integrated into our daily lives, societal acceptance and trust will be essential. There is a need for open dialogue, public engagement, and education to demystify these technologies and address concerns and misconceptions. Cultivating a sense of agency, understanding, and empowerment among individuals will be crucial in ensuring that human values and ethical considerations are preserved as we navigate the ever-evolving landscape of human-machine interaction.

Ethical frameworks and policy development are vital to guide the responsible development and deployment of intelligent systems. As technology advances at a rapid pace, it is important to establish clear guidelines and standards that prioritize the well-being and autonomy of individuals, address potential risks and biases, and ensure accountability and transparency. Collaboration between policymakers, technologists, ethicists, and the public is crucial to develop comprehensive frameworks that govern the use of intelligent technologies and promote their beneficial and ethical integration into society.

The future of human-machine interaction holds both great promise and complex challenges. It is up to us, as individuals and as a society, to shape this future in a way that fosters innovation, enhances human capabilities, and upholds our values. By embracing a human-centred approach, incorporating diverse perspectives, and proactively addressing ethical considerations, we can create a future where humans and machines coexist harmoniously, augmenting our abilities, expanding our knowledge, and enriching our lives.

In conclusion, the future of human-machine interaction is filled with exciting possibilities. Augmented reality, brain-computer interfaces, societal attitudes, and ethical frameworks will shape this future. By embracing emerging technologies responsibly, fostering public engagement, and developing robust policies, we can harness the potential of human-machine collaboration to create a future that benefits individuals and society as a whole. As we embark on this journey, let us strive to uphold our values, prioritize human well-being, and ensure that the advancements in human-machine interaction contribute to a brighter and more inclusive future. Throughout, history, humans have marveled at the intricate workings of the human brain. As the seat of our consciousness, thoughts, and emotions, it is a truly remarkable organ. However, in recent times, the rise of technology has sparked a fascinating debate: can machines ever match or surpass the capabilities of the human brain? This question has led to a deeper exploration of the human brain and the potential of machines, raising both excitement and concerns about what the future may hold.

The human brain is a complex and intricate network of billions of interconnected neurons. It is divided into various regions, each with its own specialized functions. The frontal lobe, for example, is associated with decision-making and problem-solving, while the temporal lobe is involved in processing sensory information. The brain's incredible complexity allows us to think, reason, create, and experience a wide range of emotions.

The brain's functioning relies on electrical impulses and chemical signals that travel between neurons. When a thought is formed or an action is initiated, neurons communicate through a process known as synaptic transmission. This intricate dance of electrical and chemical signals allows for the seamless integration of sensory information, memory retrieval, and the execution of complex tasks.

One of the fascinating aspects of the human brain is its ability to learn and adapt. Through a process known as neuroplasticity, the brain can reorganize its neural connections and modify its structure based on experiences and environmental influences. This remarkable plasticity allows us to acquire new skills, learn from mistakes, and continually grow and develop throughout our lives.

In contrast, machines are designed and programmed to perform specific tasks based on predefined algorithms. Early computing machines were limited in their capabilities, relying on simple logic and mathematical calculations. However, with the advent of artificial intelligence (AI) and machine learning, machines have made significant strides in emulating human intelligence.

Machine learning, a subfield of AI, involves training machines to learn from data and make predictions or decisions without explicit programming. Neural networks, inspired by the structure and functioning of the human brain, have played a crucial role in advancing machine learning algorithms. These networks consist of interconnected nodes, or artificial neurons, that process and transmit information to arrive at desired outputs.

Deep learning, a subset of machine learning, has propelled the field forward by enabling machines to process vast amounts of data and extract complex patterns and insights. This has led to breakthroughs in areas such as image recognition, natural language processing, and autonomous vehicles. Machines have demonstrated remarkable capabilities, surpassing human performance in certain specific tasks.

However, despite these advancements, machines still fall short in replicating the full range of human cognitive abilities. While machines excel at tasks that require vast data processing, accuracy, and speed, they often lack the nuanced understanding, creativity, and adaptability of the human brain. The human brain's ability to make intuitive leaps, think creatively, and navigate complex and uncertain situations is still unmatched by machines.

Moreover, human intelligence encompasses more than just cognitive abilities. It includes emotional intelligence, social awareness, and ethical considerations. Our emotions play a significant role in decision-making, motivation, and interpersonal interactions. Machines, lacking emotions and subjective experiences, struggle to understand and respond appropriately to complex human emotions and social dynamics.

Consciousness, another mysterious aspect of human intelligence, remains a subject of philosophical and scientific inquiry. While machines can process information and carry out tasks, they do not possess subjective awareness or a sense of self. The question of whether machines can ever achieve true consciousness or self-awareness remains unanswered.

The debate between human intelligence and machine intelligence is not about pitting one against the other but rather about understanding their unique strengths and limitations. Machines have undoubtedly made impressive advancements and continue to do so, transforming various industries and opening new possibilities. However, the human brain's complexity, adaptability, and capacity for creativity and empathy remain unparalleled.

Rather than viewing human intelligence and machine intelligence as competitors, there is an opportunity for synergy and collaboration. By harnessing the strengths of both humans and machines, we can achieve remarkable feats. Humans can provide the context, ethical considerations, and creative insights, while machines can process vast amounts of data, identify patterns, and assist in decision-making.

Already, we see examples of successful human-machine collaborations in various fields. In healthcare, intelligent systems assist doctors in diagnosing diseases and recommending treatment options, combining the expertise of medical professionals with the processing power of machines. In manufacturing, robots work alongside human workers, augmenting their capabilities and enhancing productivity. These collaborations demonstrate the potential for humans and machines to work harmoniously, leveraging each other's strengths for greater efficiency and innovation.

As the field of artificial intelligence continues to evolve, it is crucial to address the ethical considerations that arise. Privacy, algorithmic bias, job displacement, accountability, and transparency are among the key ethical challenges that need to be carefully navigated. Establishing robust regulations, responsible development practices, and ongoing dialogue is essential to ensure the ethical use of machine intelligence and protect human rights and well-being.

Looking ahead, the future of human-machine interaction holds tremendous potential. Emerging technologies such as augmented reality and brain-computer interfaces offer exciting possibilities for enhancing human capabilities and experiences. However, societal attitudes, education, and ethical frameworks will shape how these technologies are integrated into our lives.

In conclusion, the comparison between the human brain and machines is a fascinating exploration that raises profound questions about intelligence, consciousness, and the future of humanity. While machines continue to make remarkable strides in emulating certain aspects of human intelligence, they still fall short in replicating the full range of human cognitive abilities. Instead of viewing machines as rivals, we have the opportunity to harness their strengths and work together to unlock new frontiers of innovation and progress. By embracing a human-centred approach, addressing ethical considerations, and nurturing collaboration between humans and machines, we can shape a future where technology serves as a powerful tool for human advancement and well-being.

As we delve deeper into the capabilities of machines, we begin to question the limitations of our own intelligence. We witness the rise of artificial intelligence, driven by powerful algorithms and vast computational power. Neural networks and deep learning algorithms show remarkable potential in emulating human cognitive processes, from recognizing patterns to understanding natural language. The emergence of machine learning opens up new frontiers in problem-solving, data analysis, and decision-making. We witness machines surpassing human abilities in areas such as chess, poker, and image recognition, challenging our understanding of what it means to be intelligent.

Yet, as we explore the landscape of machine intelligence, we encounter complex debates. Can machines truly replicate human creativity? Can they possess emotional intelligence and empathy? What about consciousness itself? These questions probe the essence of what it means to be human and raise ethical considerations. The book delves into these philosophical inquiries, engaging readers in thought-provoking discussions about the nature of intelligence and the potential implications of artificial intelligence.

However, rather than framing the discussion as a competition between human and machine intelligence, "Beyond Intelligence" embraces the concept of synergy and collaboration. It envisions a future where humans and machines work together harmoniously, leveraging their respective strengths to solve complex problems and drive innovation. Real-world examples of successful human-machine collaborations illuminate the transformative potential of such partnerships. From healthcare to manufacturing, education to creative industries, we witness the power of collaboration as human expertise intertwines with machine intelligence to achieve extraordinary outcomes.

The book also delves into the social impact of human-machine collaboration. It acknowledges the concerns surrounding job displacement and inequality and emphasizes the need for inclusive access to intelligent technologies. It calls for the development of policies and initiatives that ensure equitable distribution of the benefits of collaboration and provide individuals with the necessary skills to thrive in a changing landscape. By addressing these societal challenges, we can pave the way for a future where human-machine collaboration contributes to a more prosperous and inclusive society.

Ethical considerations loom large in the book's exploration of human-machine interaction. Privacy, algorithmic bias, accountability, transparency, and the risks associated with relying too heavily on machines for decision-making are all examined through an ethical lens. The book emphasizes the importance of establishing robust frameworks and guidelines that prioritize human values, protect individual rights, and ensure that the use of intelligent technologies aligns with ethical standards. By proactively addressing these ethical challenges, we can navigate the evolving landscape of human-machine interaction responsibly and ethically.

As we gaze into the future, the book presents a vision of human-machine interaction that holds immense promise. Emerging technologies such as augmented reality and brain-computer interfaces offer tantalizing possibilities for enhancing human capabilities and transforming various domains of society. The book highlights the importance of nurturing public engagement, cultivating societal acceptance, and fostering ongoing dialogue about the future of human-machine collaboration. By embracing a human-centered approach, we can shape a future where technology serves as a tool for human progress, empowering individuals, and amplifying our collective intelligence.

Ultimately, "Beyond Intelligence: Exploring the Boundaries of Human and Machine Minds" leaves readers with a sense of wonder and anticipation. It ignites their curiosity about the evolving landscape of human intelligence and the potential of machine intelligence. It challenges preconceived notions, sparks introspection, and invites readers to contemplate the ethical, social, and philosophical implications of this rapidly evolving field. It encourages individuals and society as a whole to approach the future with open minds, responsible stewardship, and a commitment to fostering a symbiotic relationship between human and machine minds.

As we close the final pages of the book, we are left with a profound realization: the exploration of human and machine intelligence is not merely an intellectual exercise, but a journey that will shape the future of our species. It is a journey that requires careful navigation, mindful consideration of ethical implications, and a commitment to human values. "Beyond Intelligence" invites us to embrace the opportunities and challenges that lie ahead, reminding us that the boundaries of human and machine minds are fluid and that our capacity for curiosity, empathy, and innovation can guide us towards a future where human potential reaches new heights in collaboration with intelligent machines.